Black Snowflakes

Snowflakes

Smothering
A Torch

or how to talk to your veteran - a primer

Ryan Stovall

Black Snowflakes Smothering A Torch

or How To Talk To Your Veteran

A Primer

Ryan Stovall

woodhall press

Woodhall Press
Norwalk, CT

Woodhall Press, 81 Old Saugatuck Road, Norwalk, CT 06855
WoodhallPress.com
Copyright © 2022 Ryan Stovall

Cover design: Jessica Wright
Layout artist: Rysz Merey

Library of Congress Cataloging-in-Publication Data available

ISBN 978-1-954907-27-0   (paper: alk paper)
ISBN 978-1-954907-28-7   (electronic)

First Edition
Distributed by Independent Publishers Group
(800) 888-4741

Printed in the United States of America

frame:

(as a verb)

- to devise, invent, fabricate (a rule, story, theory, etc.); to contrive; to put together, fashion, compose; to put into words, express; to formulate

- to form or construct (a thought, a concept, an idea, etc.) in the mind; to conceive; to imagine.

(as a noun)

- something that confers structure; a structure composed of parts joined or fitted together that supports or encloses something, ie, a building, ship, piece of furniture, etc; a surrounding structure in which something, esp. a picture, pane of glass, etc., is set.

- a section of narrative which encloses the main narrative or narratives of a text, esp. one which sets in context the primary narrative.

- a mental or emotional disposition or state (eg., frame of mind).

primer:

- a preparatory coat on previously unpainted metal to prevent the development of rust; a cosmetic applied to improve coverage and lasting effect

- a cap or cylinder which responds to friction or electricity to ignite the charge in a cartridge or explosive; a small pump for pumping fuel to prime an engine

- an elementary textbook used to teach children to read; a small introductory book on any subject; something which serves as a first means of instruction

- the first, the foremost (obsolete, rare)

Contents

Dukkha

Gondollied

Warning:

This is not a book of poetry.

No. Black Snowflakes is a primer, a manual for teaching those who have experienced war and those who have not how to converse.

To do so, the text highlights specifics of the veteran experience and explores some of the varied human reactions to war. But since at its most foundational level this book posits the theory that many of the problems veterans face reintegrating into society come not from the traumas of war but from qualities inherent to the American way of life itself, more is needed. So in attempting to grapple with this more fundamental issue, societal and cultural values ranging from our still ubiquitous patriarchy to our unquestioned consumerism are considered in these pages as well.

As a means of facilitating dialogue, between those who've returned from war and those who nominally sent them, Black Snowflakes serves as an invaluable new starting point for both civilians seeking to understand and veterans attempting to explain.

For Doug

Gershom[1]

---

[1] I have become a stranger in a strange land
Exodus 2:22

Manhattan

having shot children
we return to too many faces
shuffling sundown drenched streets
brown black or pale
sweating
some seem accusatory

but soon under towers' shadows
we see we're still okay
cause of the few
out on Hudson's water
not a one
is walking on it

Two, or More

he's Hescoed in, barricaded
behind his lectern, microphone
and dark horn rimmed glasses
an owl mumbling inanities
in place of poems
spewing cold
a broken pipe's sewer gush
unintelligible stuff, cock-eyed diction
butter soft, incapable
of slicing to the bleeding quick
either intellect
or soul

I'd need two beers, I hush,
to stick my dick in this.
Bare minimum. My Army
buddy nods, rolls her eyes.

finally
it stops
and to close, a second owl stands
drums wings, clicks beak
and hoots the first's pure courage
(context—self examination)
admiring at length the nerve required
to poetry
and to quote
so unflinchingly contemplate
the craven void within us all

I pick at an Afghanistan shard
stuck *just* beneath the skin
until my left leg bleeds my heart's disgust
at sheltered ivory tower fools

Winning[2]

I don't want to win the old way any more

we used to kick doors down
or blow them in
no huffing or puffing though
by the hair on anyone's chin
then we'd all come running in
and shoot anybody stupid enough
to still be holding a gun a knife a baby or
any other weapon
brutal yes
and mistakes were sometimes made
but clean simple and direct
and most definitely an end

he won't have the guts to try that again
we'd say
looking at a corpse blown open
eviscerated thin
blue sausage-link intestines spilling out
secret and as embarrassing to us
as paramedics cutting off soiled undies

he just Houdini'ed on us
we'd joke
straight up disappeared
where'd he go?
well someone would say
pointing
some of him is over there
but where's the rest?
I've got three fingers
and a chunk of skull with scalp and hair

[2] I shall win at the odds
Hamlet 5:2

someone would call out from a dusty corner
an excited prospector spying something beautiful
and rare
and look
he even made it to the ceiling
he's coming back down now though
drip   drip   drip   drip
He's your grandma's glasses now
we'd say
he's everywhere and nowhere all at once

last mistake he'll ever make
we'd quip
looking down at sockets missing eyes
and thighs
blown open like exploded footballs
muscles raw exposed and bloody as a steak
strips of cloth and shards of door
splintered slimy bone
and just plain grit
all ground into his leg meat
the filthiest of hamburger
we'd sing
when we come a knockin
your house will be rockin
when we come a knockin
your house will be rockin
don't answer the door
cause we're gonna come right in
don't answer the door dude
someone would advise
squatting down beside our friend
and his empty fleshy sockets
and disintegrated thighs

yes

very honest
very simple
clean direct and oh so final
and we called that winning

but I don't sleep much these days
not with all these memories of winning
up and running races through my head
at two a.m.
my lowest ebb
so I don't want to win that way anymore
no
if it will help me rest
I want to win the New way
the urban stylish civilized way
the learned pretentious academic way
the polite two-faced ingratiating way
the slap you on the shoulder
shoot you in the back way
if it will keep my memories at bay
then I will smile and smile
and be a villain

Black Snowflakes Smothering a Torch

we return red in the face as velvet lingerie
raped
smuggling a man inside our bodies
literally
a true believer who thrust his bloody bony bits
cuticles adipose and hairy skin
beneath our hairy skin
when he blew himself apart
and we're taken care of
which means returned to these united states
for surgeries extracting all injected bits
and first rate care for blood-borne pathogens

or more often we return
more literally
more republican conventionally
raped
cornered in a conex office
held down inside a plywood b hut
pinned within a BFV's unyielding troop compartment
and shoved bloody by some Bradley dismount's
angry dangling bits
and we're taken care of
which means returned
item unwanted
in disgrace
to these true-believer and oh so just united states
because surprise!
even though the shoving's long since stopped
we find ourselves still cornered by a hostile trooper
some dismount's blown inside our own compartment

and once shipped back in disgrace

to these oh so masculine united states
we begin taking the lord's name in vain
saying fuck the goddamn judging church
and its goddamn sanctity of life
jesus wanna climb down
off his fubar roman phalus
and raise this child up?

when he doesn't
thanks to free will and the supremest court
of these hypocritical united states
we choose not to be a smuggling berth
for our injected rape trophy

afterwards
we call the Bradley dismount
to tell him his inblown it's been given first rate care
in truest bluest Army style
which means scraped away peeled off and vacuumed out
med bagged tagged and incinerated
sent back to some oh so just masculine deity—
Compunctionless, the patron saint of rapists—
and we say you're welcome
now go fuck yourself

but literally fucked or no
when we return we're whipped
tired to death and jealous of dead friends
who came home boxed and metal floor loaded
on chilly C-17s
white sterile lights paling the cheap thin flags
draped across their boxes

jealous
that's right

so we return on Facebook
draping ourselves in friends and statuses
until we realize most people post mere outtakes
taken from lives lived mostly none too well
and that the whole goddamn scrolling nut roll
engenders a hate suffering and distance
far darker than Marines
gang banging teenage Filipina prostitutes

it's true

then
feeling gypped by and jealous of the dead
and driven to set the record straight
regarding antisocial media
we zealots prop our minds and bodies up
seemingly so they can stand
as proof that sometimes
dead really is better

or
driven to distraction by
the shelf-life shiny plastic
splayed across the facebooker
limp and pathetic as the wide-splayed legs
of a teenage hooker
we find ourselves driven
to taking the lord's name in vain
because you see
despite maybe having killed
a few of the wrong people
we still return boasting hearts beaten purple
and impaled outside our chests
and mount red white and bullshit floats
to barge between thick screaming lines
of you flag-waving bright young things

and we begin taking Prozac
and the lord's name in vain
because what we realize
that the flag-wearing four year olds
and their parents
don't
is that some of us up there floating
returned boasting heart beats
like epileptic tap dancers
that when safely locked inside a bathroom
we scream insults at every surface
shined enough to show us
our own bath-salted faces
that despite having returned
our twisting hearts and melted faces
mean from here on out
we'll never mount anything
more sexy than a bunted parade float
and that instead we'll find ourselves
cornered and serially mounted
held down by gangs of cardiologists
pinned by surgeons made of plastic
every one of them drip-tip eager
for a piece of that good ol' melted pussy

some return orchiotomized
literally lacking testes
and live out lives spent smuggling
implanted plastic plums
and some return still packing their organics
but hoping to outlive labels such as Nutless
Pogue
Fobbit
War Tourist
Dead Weight
Hajji Target

Desk Patroller
Behind the Wire Skulking Coward Mother Fucker
some of which they find themselves unable to outlive
because as it turns out
they deserve every appellation
albatrossed around
their spindly good for nothing necks

but nuts or none
even some of us pipe-hitting HALO studs
return afraid of everything
from sudden movements
to failure
from disapproval
to dissecting aortas
to displaying cowardice
or courage
since courage we discover has
in these pusserific United States
become as popular as the big ol' scarlet A
branded on the brows
of our pinned down and shoved bloody sisters
but don't say so to our first responders
the ones you all so vibrantly support
but so adamantly refuse to pay

so either we find our silent selves
so full of fear and trembling
that we return making lists
so we can make amends for each mistake we've ever made
so we can make amends to spouses who
our cocks and trigger fingers have made nervous
or
those of us unhitched
and still packing real testes
with no amends to make

return making up a medley
of bullshit
to set all you bright young things atrembling
and get laid

in either case
when we return
we make pacts and promises
to pack reunion halls
and drink and reminisce
in true blue PTSD style
telling half-soused war stories
that cut the day to day ennui
and joyfully reinstill belief
if only for a moment
in combat's fear and trembling

and in either case
despite returning loaded down with shiny dangling medals
on the 4th we still go out and get loaded
early
so that long before we're loaded onto floats
and paraded
we're crying in our fears
and staking the Lord Sname in vain
because soused shiny or not
we know not all bright dangly bits
are created equal
are equal in merit
are equal in the eyes of men
or in the long-lashed eyes of God
whereas the barging lines of you bright young things
we blear between
won't don't or can't know
about Fobbits packing medals
about Marines spangled with stars

about our bathroom invective
about our blown off dangly bits
and plastic smuggled plums

to forget the great disparity
we get lit up
or we light up a joint
and it helps some of us to smooth
to soften or to mellow
to pastel our scarlet fire
so maybe more of us
should light up a joint
because all too often
we wind up too wound up
and end up lighting up a joint
as in a bar massage parlor or nightclub
because all we've done and seen
has veiled the human light within us
like black snowflakes smothering a torch
because all we've seen and done
has made shooting shiny humans
light us up like ardent scarlet torches
whereas drinking and/or dancing
seems too soft
too tame
too cold

some give interviews to local papers
while some give up completely
and it's only when we try repairing
our lives and reputations
that we wish upon our scars
we hadn't given in
acquiesced
hadn't been so giving
hadn't felt it so important that we prove—

despite all evidence to the contrary
despite the twisting scars marbling our twisted faces
like the fat of famined lands
despite our twisted minds
seething with a hatred of the calm and undisfigured
more befitting some outcast tribe
of vagrant club-foot dwarves
despite the black bracelets we boast in place of Rolexes
with dates and names and foreign places which
by the time of our return
half of us have twisted in half in loving rage—
we scarwish away our proving of our life desire
our passion to show we were are and can still be
alive
even in these pastel pasty
and oh so progressive
United States

because you see my bright young things
we've returned aboard the USS Regret
which toot toot toot!
should have been decommissioned
by Jesus Christ himself
but instead still barges on
and having bought a berth
and burning with our shames
and feeling burned by this christian system
eye for an eye
and the weak shall inherit
and consume the earth
because regret and shame are burning us
from the moment we make land
we're burning with impatience
to jump right off the goddamn boat
and burn said system down
and we're already to the point

of taking the lord's name
pointlessly
because while over kissing Satan's sandy taint
we go on missions gone wrong
Air Force crashtastrophes
that leave us burned by JP-8
faces-melted eyeballs-boiled burned
so that when we return
we're riding high and blind
on PRN IVs
raking our impatient spurs across the ragged ribs
of shiny Ketamine ponies

or some return as blindly righteous prigs
all set to prove their pens more potent
than ol' Ma Deuce herself
and put down bayonets for books
and go to college
to try to suss out
exactly what a snowflake is
and it's only when they're drifted in
that they recall the pleasant warmth
and wickedness
of heavy guns and killing

or determined to prove some priggish status
to some insipid Joneses
returning we put down money on a house
before we come to know
owning property
in a failing state
on a failing world
is futility in four walls

or we return to prove ourselves compassionate
so that now

when we put down the family cat
we euthanize
we kill efficiently
because we know how to shoot
and how to put down
our emotions

and knowing weapons as we do
and since our emotions
aside from sweet Mother Anger
and sick Sister Despair
have long ago
been dealt a graceless *coup de grâce*
while some return to prove the sword's inferiority
and thereby usher in
the meek's hostile takeover
we true cat mercy killers
scoff at all such
clichéd ivory tower bullshit
take our vows
and marry Mother Anger
and then
after taking the lord's name—
Mary mother of god
are you absolutely sure you didn't just get laid?
seriously
because all the hopeless longing
for plastic shit and teenage hookers
splayed across this nut roll scrolling facebooker
is the selfsame desire
the church engenders in heaven
and manipulates through hell
and all that desperate longing
seems pretty goddamn human
Mary—
after taking the lord's name in vain

a few more times
for good measure
and because fuck her anyway
after our nuptials we stand
hand in hand with Mother Anger
scoop up our swords
and ventilate our skulls

because you see
my bright young things
returning to find ourselves unable
to distinguish a handshake
from an arm bar
or an insurgent
from a six-year-old cookie salesman
we're suffocating
beneath the burden of explaining
beneath the stories that explain
but which we find ourselves unable to tell
beneath the stories we have found
but which we find ourselves unable to tell
worth a damn
until ultimately
unable to tell history
from truth or fact or story
we find ourselves entirely unable
to find our selves
and find ourselves relegated
to writing clever poetry
that will never pierce our shroud
and we're bitter
because others return writing daggers
earning Stegner fellowships
winning the National Book Award
although as it turns out
even these latter

have grown rather accustomed
to taking the lord's name in vain

but jesus christing it or no—
I walked on ink-black oil once
does that count?—
most of us return
penning nothing but operation orders
planning missions to the post office
and unable or unwilling to self ventilate
via nine millimeter trepanation
most frequently we find ourselves
merely marking time
crouching in dark corners
caressing our swords
and muttering dark words
to our trembling unable selves

understand my bright young things
motivation to self harm
can well from many springs
we might return unsure
having to knock at our own front doors
because the lock won't turn and we haven't heard
from our wives
in four months
and not knowing whether she and the children
are dead
or if she's just fucking someone else
and not knowing which we'd prefer to be the case
what we do know is
four months spent trying to kill people
some right some wrong
without knowing
with a great big question mark hanging over our marital
          status
has been a bit of a strain

some of us return expecting a child
and some expecting our wife
to be looking forward to expecting a child
while some of us simply expect our wife
to be present with our child
because we're expecting
looking forward to
hoping
we'll have someone we can expect to listen
when we explain why we've returned
expectorating dust
dried fecal matter
burned fat cells
how we paused to watch eight little brown boys playing
soccer in the dust
how they'd laid down two piles of brown human shit
to serve as goal posts
how all of it
dust kids and shit
blew into the air in a fist of black fire
then sucked down into our rose petal pink lungs
so that no matter whether we've returned
with our shit together or our shit in a sling
shitting the bed or unable to shit at all
without first checking the shitter
for pressure plates
regardless
we're all coughing shit
from our no longer rosy pink petal lungs

but despite all the shit we've seen
done
killed
inhaled
and coughed up
a few of us still start loving families

after we return
or start a career in defense contracting
to fund our loving families
or start up therapy
before defense contracting
or
despite our symptoms screaming
we *should* start therapy
before defense contracting
we start defense contracting
because a
shrinks are expensive
and b
actual mercenary work
in which you get actual money
to shoot actual people(!)
and which unlike therapy
we think might actually help
is illegal
but we figure contracting
might be a close second
might still be beneficial
might help ease us down
dull our fires
smooth us out

but thanks to this self prescribed
penny-pinching PTSD treatment
before long we're blowing up
at the loving families we've started
over things as life or death
as how our four year old slams the bathroom door
before blowing up the shitter
as life or death
as how our wife forgets
to put the flag up for the postman

the morning we renew our subscription
to Angry Dickhead Monthly

then
once we realize we're blowing up
we take desperate measures
we stop defense contracting
we stop marking time in dark corners
and instead start blowing up our bridges
our rationale being
self ostracization
will keep sweet Mother Anger
from nursing bruises
onto our wives and four year olds
onto anyone besides
our desperate trembling selves

because
understand this
my bright young things
either we return struggling with PTSD
or we return enjoying it
because even when we do return to seeming domesticity
to flipping animal-shaped pancakes
for our four year olds
we still start flipping out
every time we're flipping through
old Army stuff
and come across old letters
diaries
combat pictures
our hearts accelerate
hands and assholes clench
and once again we start to feel
as invincible and dangerous
as virile young gods

there is a middle ground
some return not disordered
per se
but merely wistful
wishing someone would listen
wishing we ourselves had listened
to our parents
whose thing for pacifistic consumerism
as it turns out
has more or less ruined the fucking earth
to our priests
who as it turns out
had a real penchant for peace and wisdom
and for altar boys
to our Boy Scout leader
who as it turns out
had real knowledge of field craft
and of sucking Boy Scout scrotum
to our dickhead gym teacher
who as it turns out
himself returned from Vietnam
taking the lord's name in vain
and wishing someone would listen
so as it turns out
of all of them
he will listen

understand
there's vast variance in how we are when we return
because
we might return having rolled our ankles
stepping off the ramp of a C-17
in Germany
in too much of a hurry to grab a beer
and drink a hooker
in the local whore house

or *Puff*
or we might return having rolled our ankles
jumping from a twelve foot wall
in Fallujah
scrambling to get out
before some fucking zealot pulled the plug
on forty pounds of crazy
wired to his chest
and made the whole house
go *poof!*

we might return with a deep appreciation
for drill sergeants
whose training saved us
or with a deep appreciation
for nothing besides fickle luck
and for taking the lord's name in vain
but for every one who does return with a
deep appreciation for life
another has grown murderously sick
of all such mindless clichés
and returns with a deep appreciation
for profiling
because if it's dressed like a woman
but walks like a man
it's that suicide bomber in the niqab
that she-man martyr whose halting strut
sent half our squad home
missing not just half our brittle teeth
but half our solid jutting jaw bones
so that we come to know a deep appreciation
for chewing
wanting nothing so desperately
as to bite into a good ol' fashion
buttery
America on the cob

and even with mastication
now blown toothless and impossible
we still want to bite
and by way of mental masturbation
daydream of breaking jaws
so we can chew out the rubbery tongues
of every American who warbles
if you don't stand behind our troops
feel free to stand in front of them
and all such rectally vacuous clichés

and thanks to the suffocating prevalence
of all such sad clichés in these Benighted States
we return trusting no one
who herself hasn't tongued Satan's gritty taint
and returned telling truth
and spitting sand
which means we only trust each other
and dogs
because a dog will save your life
in a cinderblock house
where the stairs are wired
and the looneys have built-in machine gun nests
hatching PKMs
into every hallway

so we return different
some more so than others
or we return with differences
we're determined to settle with others
either determined to make a difference
or determining we shouldn't have returned
different the same otherwise or at all
because maybe now we're different
but for the sake of sweet purple-weeping Christ
that doesn't mean we're willing to settle

for tame pastels
and mellowed fires
and besides
as far as we can tell
now that we've returned
it's America that's different
but either way
things just aren't the same between us
the sex just isn't as good
since only some of us
managed to cum home
to this new America

and when we are permitted[3]
to return to this rank meadow's rank wind
and smashed grasses
it's only when we're properly relieved
as if we're property of a mind bound in chaos
and then
finding relief at our return
and finding it thankfully still permitted
we relieve ourselves
spill our hot thankful piss
between this meadow's cold uncaring blades
speckling this place of first permission
this tottering
already half forgotten
self fellating homage
to all that's cancerous rotten and ruining

we're disenchanted
my bright young things
and begin taking the lord's name in vain
but even when we do
some return
and begin taking a new interest in Catholicism

[3] After Robert Duncan

and take to quoting Latin
and positively french kissing God
but unfaithfully
it's a different God now
hers isn't the same pious tongue
we were all sucking
when we went over

and speaking of sucking tongue
some of us return sickened to the point of gagging
by the arousal we as veterans
now arouse
give rise to
trigger
because having dead friends say you're not to blame
when they cum visit you in bed
is about as sexy as deep throating
God's pious *lingua villosa nigra*

and some of us
having killed the wrong people
return crying and unable to respond
to mindless people's mindless thank yous for our service
or we're unable to cry
until the dam breaks
and then we're unable to stop
or we're unable to sleep
or maybe
merely unable to dream
but a lucky few of us do dream
of night HALO jumps under gentle stars
drifting down through warm clear skies
with low winds whispering across
the soft dessert sands that slumber far below
and waking up
discover we're rock hard

and cum and cum and cum
as though in the spirit of our training
we're trying to fuck our wives or husbands
to death
but more often
we return to discover dead faces
have swum between us and lust
or love
and we become unable
the Big Unable
and we begin whispering
to our uncooperative dicks
accusing them of desertion
in the vagina of the enemy
of being disrespectful
unwilling or unable to stand up
and look us in the eye

because you see my bright young things
for every one of us who returns
dreaming himself hard on HALO
or on a fresh piece of ass
quite a few of us return dreaming of a fresh corpse
that five minutes before was a friend
warning us to look sharp
pay attention
stop dreaming
and after too many iterations
waking too slopped in stinking sweat
we become unwilling or unable
to risk such ungentle sleep
and then
unable to let lust speak
we're left wondering
how will love cum
and we discover a lust for death

that leaves us wondering exactly
what the dead see in *our* faces

so we return sleepless and watch
in red-rimmed round-eyed disbelief
as Syria moves to Germany
and Italy becomes Africa
and we're called Nazis
by insulated snowflakes
who've never stepped outside
America's freezer unit strip malls
cold storage strip clubs
and ice bucket beer halls
we're called fascists
because we speak up
because we like the idea
of a country being free to speak up
and to have its own culture
instead of someone else's
the way murderous whore America
having eradicated the previous tenants
is pretty much stuck with
and also we're so labeled we assume
because hey man
these are the puritanical Benighted States
and it's common knowledge we've become
rather prone to taking the Lord's name in vain

so dreaming what we've seen
and sometimes while awake
vice versa
too often we return and dive back in
training and prepping for the next mission
and although it's never clear exactly
what that might be
regardless

a conex box buried on the back forty
stuffed with guns medicine and toiletries
for the apocalypse
sure seems like a good idea
given our dreams
and given what we've returned from

or
having escaped the proverbial woods
the jungle
the wild west
Sleepy fuckin' Hollow
we dive right back into the nearest woods
because
hiding out in Maine Montana or Alaska
sure seems like a good idea
given our dreams
and given what we've returned to

or as an alternative to being slandered
prepping
or hiding out
those of us returning as heroes in our own heads
deluded
or with some strange righteous streak
upon returning
immediately return to fighting
against Assad
AQIM
ISIS
or even elephant poachers in the South African bush
and we do so despite our knowing
upon our return from such combat safaris
we'll be prosecuted as terrorists ourselves
because in order to combat slavery
child rape

genocide
andor elephantine extinction
we've fought and killed and used explosives
and sometimes
heaven forbid
have even taken the Lord's name in vain
plus we know that as an added bonus
some of us will return from hunting humans in the bush
with the real African ju-ju
and you don't fuck with the real African ju-ju
because even before we're prosecuted
we know those GI parasites
will strip seventy pounds
from our GI one-eighty frames
leaving us prison camp thin
long before we're even sent to see
Camp Leavenworth's delights

but most of us
disinclined to self identify as heroes
disinclined to believe in heroes
or in self identification
or in pretty much anything
return and merely watch
mortified shamed and embarrassed
as these flamboyant righteous morons
eat their just desserts
and we just shake our heads
in distrustful disbelief

but whether heroes
self identified or otherwise
or mortified
regardless we return tattooed
then watch as the whole fuckin' country
eighteen to eighty

goes sideways and starts sitting for ink
watch as a few of us return and ink
no-shit-there-I-was books
and movie deals
but those are usually SEALS
and the books
are usually crap
while the movies
go figure
are usually propaganda
so who gives a shit
but despite our knowing
before our lives go sideways
we watch those SEALs' movies
and laugh ourselves sideways
at Hollywood
and by extension
America
and at those SEALs
and by extension
America

but setting SEALs aside
we return thinking the Army
hadn't been that bad
compared to the Marines
and as for the Air Force
well my bright young things
let's just say that some of us
Army and Marines both
having lost friends in crashtastic Air Force fuck ups
return planning to dick punch
the first C-17 navigator
we catch bragging about how he
earned
his hazard pay

and speaking of Marines
we return having learned
you never hand a Marine a knife[4]
and tell him to cut your uniform's ankle hem
while you lay down suppressive fire
because whether you need to stuff Kerlex
in your bleeding knee or not
he might be a Marine
but he's still a kid
and he's wired tight
and amped up
and he'll default to fulfilling his Prime Directive
and wanting to kill kill kill
he'll try using your tibia
as a cutting board
and trust me
your leg with just the bullet in it
isn't bleeding *that* bad

and we've also learned
to never tell that same Marine[5]
to lay down suppressive fire
and move out of the way
so you can bandage your own bleeding leg
and then bandage your bleeding friend
because that Marine will only hear the first half
of your order
before he'll default to fulfilling his Prime Directive
and wanting to kill kill kill
he'll pull his stupid fucking pistol
turn it sideways
like in some stupid fucking movie
and pump fifteen nine mil rounds
into a distant hillside
while screaming
while still straddling your wounded friend

[4] 0730 on 29 July, 2009 (2200 on the evening of the 28th in D.C., 1900 in the Skagit Valley). Near Arawu, Surobi District.
[5] About twenty minutes later

so you can't say
or do
or think
anything
except how fucking stupid he is

and from this experience
and from also hearing later
that this young Marine
was given a Silver Star
for what(ever it was) he did that day
we also learn
how you carry yourself in combat
matters half as much
as how you carry yourself in the chow hall
when other people
the ones who gift Silver Stars
are watching
just like with civilian jobs
but with bullets

and
not necessarily still speaking of Marines
when we return
we learn lesbians
with enough balls to live openly
in the 90s
in America
land of liberty
tolerance
and a four-hundred year old value system
the middle ages has called about
and wants back
are some of the few civilians
whose courage we respect

and
still not necessarily speaking of Marines
we also learn to retrain our minds
to not call guys we're working with Ass Pirates
Dick Lickers
Horn Blowers
Cum Buckets
Gum Cuzzlers
Cock Holsters
Gerbil Enthusiasts
Shrimp Fishermen
anymore
because all of a sudden
some of the guys we're working with
are openly gay
and as it turns out
they're pretty good guys

and one more thing that isn't necessarily about Marines
but might be
when we return we learn we're disrespected[6]
by the angry, hurting Marine brothers
of men who died in our care

so we return and learn
and get down to business
or sometimes
if we're lucky
we return
and get down with you bright young things
either way
we return down airport escalators
to waiting families
and boy scout troops
and troop greeters
and saluting state troopers

[6] 27 July 2013

and all you giddy bright young things
but many of us gliding down those perpetually flowing
       stairs
are down an eye
a leg
a hand
or dick
and some of us are somber
and some of us are laughing
not because of any particular gravitas
or because anything is particularly funny
but because everything is fucked
except for the dickless guys of course
who
aside from escalator rides
will never get down again
and we begin to giggle uncontrollably
which thankfully
unfortunately?
whatever
makes it impossible
for the cheruby boy scouts gaggling nearby to hear
how in between our red-faced giggles
we've given up even trying to stop ourselves
from taking the lord's name in vain

Chihiro[7]

[7] "thousand questions"

Zen? (*a koan*)

if a coffee cup
        an oversized metal travel mug

is dropped
        bounces between several pairs of sturdy boots

and slides
        out the open door of an American helicopter

hovering above
        the dusty streets of Quetta[8]

spewing droplets
        a chrome meteor

spinning down
        shining through the sunlight

filling cool
        desert morning air

gathering a
        thousand feet of speed before

striking a
        child on a bicycle

splitting her
        head like a dark haired pumpkin

---

[8] June 2015. I know it's been a while, but try to remember—
where were you? What were you up to?

whacked by
    an axe

does it make a sound
    in America?

A Fine Point

will you dedicate your self?
will you kill kill kill for country?
shall *I* voice a dozen dozen questions
not so openly pronounced?
shall *I* interrogate the process?

no
I agreed and signed
many times on many dotted lines
then fulfilled my contract

but then
my obligation complete
and having sensed the pointlessness
and failed at pointing out the senselessness
in what we've done
did
do
and will continue doing
I got out

but they're not the same
the senselessness and pointlessness
what we've done did do had at its roots a *point*
and when flower blooms as root intends
all can and should bask in its light
it's in our application's fronds
senseless leaf mold thrives

for example
I was working medevac
standing by at a Dakar beach resort
a hotel perched on the sandy nipple-tip of Africa

the milk of which for centuries was slaves

going to the beach
the tv in the lobby announced Bin Laden's death[9]
I reveled late
drinking my Flag until fully unfurled
prone and sandy on that same bitch
that launched a thousand sorrow-slammed ships
lit up and lit up by the news
that brightest of pitch blossoms
had survived all mold
and
although almost ten years later
matured and borne full fruit

[9] 2 May 2011. A death-of-Kennedy or 9/11 moment (for some of us). Where you were when you heard the news?

American Weddings

why do american weddings almost never get bombed?

because after an early morning knot tying
americans eat celebratory bowls
of Multi-Grain Cheerios™
instead of shooting AK-47s into the air

sure
that
and they don't get married in afghanistan[10]

---

[10] Haska Meyna, Nangahar, 6 July 2008, Wech Baghtu, Kanda-
har, 3 November 2008, and Musa Qala, Helmand, 22 November
2019. Where was your wedding? When? Any airstrikes?

I Helped[11]

they claimed you were ten
but no American would have guessed seven
scant food had left you stunted, your bones brittled
and now your dusky brown fragility lay shattered
a broken clay pot beneath a crisp white sheet

they claimed a stone wall caved in
but how could we know if that was true?
there are so many ways a girl child can be broken
in the desiccated mountains bordering Afghanistan

they claimed you were in pain
and tears did pool in your eyes
but when I sank my stare in those soft dark wells
I saw a plea beyond your current mangled state

they claimed you were deserving of my help
so I delved until I found a vein
drew up morphine from a vial
then threw one last look
into your wretched eyes
seeking confirmation
or encouragement
maybe absolution?
and pushed ten times your dose[12]

[11] 5 November 2009, COP Najil, Mehtar Lam. Where were *you*?
What were you up to?

[12] Hippocrates—who never worked the Hindu Kush—and his
oath can straight up fuck off.

Medic Guilt

If I tell of terror
must I also admit shame?
Shall I say I have lain spread-eagled in a breeze-torn verdant
      field
my boots to a solitary rock
my eyes squeezed shut while snap-crack bullets
clipped the wholesome grass
and dropped their tidbit stalks onto my Mich?

I have seen soldiers go wild-eyed
when bark sprayed by bullets from a pine
when limbs and needles showered from a pine
spattered across their sweating shoulders where they
crouched below
and I have found men curled behind stacked-stone walls
as if the womb were present in the furrows of a plow

I have smelt the death sweat pouring from a friend
have known *I* lead him there
have known that in my fear I failed him
have known behind the rock I failed him
that when I failed to immediately open my eyes
and rise
I failed him.[13]

[13] 29 July 2009, again. For The Cat, and all those he left behind.
I'm sorry, Dougie Fresh.

Kohelet[14]

[14] What has been will be again,
and what has been done will be done again;
there is nothing new under the sun
                    Ecclesiastes 1:9

I have seen all the things
that are done under the sun,
and have found them all to be futile,
a pursuit of the wind.
                    Ecclesiastes 1:14

Barracks Living

let me explain it for you
in a nutshell
barracks living is being blinded
by automatic motion-sensored lights
when shuffling across the hall to piss
at two a.m.
unbidden erection tucked
like an angry pistol
up into pjs' elastic waistband
beneath long concealing t-shirt
restrained
to avoid tent pitching
should you
by somnolent unluck
lurch into a zombied tête-à-tête

The Embassy Voyeur

even Dali
could not convey onto canvas
the flickering shadows and lights
how they played so desperately
across the under side
of the pool cover

he might however
have depicted the mind
of the young boy trapped beneath
legs tangled skin-cutting tight
in a submerged water volleyball net

he might have shown the terror
the blood-stricken eyes
wide and bulging with pain
begging help escaping
that glittering alien tomb

he might have conferred to canvas
the melting fading feeling
which passed so clear across
the boy's face
and proceeded death
and the sudden surreality of calm

I picture a work of pastels and lights
running softly to one side
like ripples on a pond disturbed
by gentle wind

but near the frame
in some unimportant corner

small insignificant yet menacing
would be I
solid defined uncontorted perhaps
save for my massive eyes
water still dripping from my hair
having dunked my head
beneath the pool cover to watch
the Iraqi pool boy drown

But By The Grace of Poor Weapons Maintenance[15]

an Afghan comes pounding down the path
pell melling it toward me
his broken boots puffing dust

and I hesitate
thinking
here is surely one of ours
a desperate straggler separated
by our ambushed swift retreat

camouflaged
still
he does not see me til I'm at his very feet
an adder warm and waiting in the dirt

he freezes too
stands mouth agape
god-big
dark
a hairy eclipsing planet
to permanently block my sun

my whole life
reduced to an instant

his malfunction
a dry click
amplified by the mere inches between his muzzle
and my ear
rips me from my horrified revery
I twist and stitch his torso groin to sternum
with one staccato burst

[15] For Rodney

You Will Lie Still[16]

lie still
breathe
RPGs and mortars blowing sparky flowered blossoms
tracers stitching rosy angles
through Atropos's felty night
all have passed you by

lie still
while they progress by feel
theirs is no rigid disciplined sweep
but a cautious ragged line of faintly moonlit silhouettes
clearing this desert killing ground

they might miss you

lie still
as blood
moonlight will show each tacky sheen
but not its source
it's splashed on rocks
on dirt
on you
and on your buddies maimed and silent

surely you've *some* chance

lie still
they're close
closer
cutting throats as they come
but Hope's butterfly still flutter floats
beside throbbing lizard Terror in your chest
so many friends are lying near they might still miss you yet

---

[16] For Durant, and Luttrell. For every soldier who's ever walked
away alone.

lie still
someone's father
brother
son
has been discovered
has failed the test
has been found out
his pleas are choked by gurgling

there's no hope of being taken prisoner

lie still
a sour smell looms over you
a rank silhouette eclipses moon
it stoops to take a closer look
nudges your forehead
with an unclean sandaled foot

lie still
let head roll limp
under prodding toe
don't breathe
don't twitch
one tell
and his dripping knife
will let your life's water
spatter this desert's dustiness

lie still
don't show your hope
he straightens and moves on
wait
then take one half
a single silent breath
wait
and then

exhale
lie still
strain your ears to ringing
voices harsh as digger's spades
striking graveyard bedrock
sound near in quiet darkness
how near are those limber tongues?
will they sweep again?

lie still
all is quiet night
no sounds no voices
gone
or simply fallen silent?
do they listen too?
wait
fight every screaming instinct
to look
to rise
to run
breathe
wait
and listen.

rise!
flee!
run stumbling in search of any friendly face!

until finally when you're back on base
guarded
safe
then
feeling nascent guilt and shame
lie when working to explain
how you alone survived

later you will lie again
when questioned closer
and upon returning home to resume your former life
when you try to tell this story to your children or your
               wife—
you will lie still

Army Brat[17]

summer's last faint breath pushes up the hill
a gentle warmth that speaks of growth
and love

there will be no other breeze
like this
until some time late
next year

the tall grass bends
embraces the breeze
the oak's leaves give up a gracious sighing
the girl's short yellow hair ruffles
a little

black clouds
gather behind the breeze
stark brutal winter
staring out of each

the girl turns and with a solemn heart
trudges down the meadow hill
that faces out
across the sea

[17] 3 October 1993, the Maine coast. For Gary Gordon and family—your sacrifice is not forgotten. DOL

The Firing Line

under the searing sun of Gao[18]
between some scrubby brush
and the last few stunted trees
at the edge of the sand
where the paved road and all life ends
a sweating line of coal-black sons
prostrate themselves upon the ground
as if to pray

all squint against the searing sun of Gao
across a swath of sand
to where a jumbled mound of smashed basalt
lies broken black and pink
at the base of a long cliff
jutting skyward like a church

this Mecca they all face
the rusting hulks of cars
not Humvees or APCs
but sedans and minivans
strewn before the rocks and left to bake
beneath the searing sun of Gao

at an order the hammers fall in unison
and the reports echo from the cliff
and join the cacophony of whining ricochets
and plinking tinny hits
rolling sharp and menacing
across the desert lying bare
under the searing sun of Gao

atop the cliff
the ghost of Mother France

[18] July 2006. *Gao* rhymes with *bow, now, how? pow!* and *cow.*

looks down on them
from the bombed and burned out remnants
of an old colonial villa
tears flowing down her peachy cheeks
to wither and parch
beneath the searing sun of Gao

Tripped Up By Mefloquine[19]

nothing was normal in Africa
for example
I had my own room in our Bamako team house
a kitchen I converted to a clinic
I slept on the floor atop a thin foam pad
but had my privacy
my teammates
more comfortably bunked
were two to a room
the night we practiced NPAs
lube
pig his nose
insert while twisting back and forth
ignore the blood and gagging
that night the Mefloquine
caught me out
melted in my mind
instead of my hand
and on my thin foam pad
I dreamt our comms guy Karl
needed fixing
I went to work with saw and scalpel
and soon amputated his torso
a clean incision
dropping everything below the solar plexus
a success
he recovered nicely
and thereafter
anytime we went from room to room
he'd link his hands above his head
making a handle by which we'd carry him
like a suitcase
we'd lug him in to dinner

[19] July 2007. For Karl Hungus.

plop him on the table's center
he'd converse as normal
while we ate

The Eternal Return of Willy Pete[20]

dusked early beneath stark cliffs
the Kabul's rising gorge roiling past
we drop white phosphorus mortar rounds
stockpiled since Vietnam

the shells trace steep bilious arcs
from thunder belching tubes
shooting up from shaded banks
into sideways glowing sun

then plummet queasy back
to crack and scorch with their old fire
much older broken rock

[20] 1830, 17 August 2008, just downstream from Naghlu Dam.

Shoot At Me

fear is watching tracers stitch
between your sniper partner[21]'s legs
when at dusk his desert BDUs
sprint the dusty road
that winds the valley
up to Sper Kunday[22]

love is hoping the Talib gunner
will notice your humvee
will decide your truck
—a lumbering behemoth of a target
compared to a single sprinting man—
is in need of stitching

[21] For the Blond Chinaman.
[22] 1830, 18 August 2008. See Wikipedia article, Uzbin Valley Ambush. Think back. How did you spend that afternoon?

The Old Man

the old afghan's breath
bitter like lees of wine
issued forth between a pair of worn decaying teeth
to reek horrible vengeance upon those closest to him
in a world that had shown neither kindness
nor pity

his face
a cracked and poorly carven countenance
dared reproach with one deep wrinkle
asked forgiveness with the next
and leered at every passersby

when I passed by[23]
patrolling
his eye coated me in an addict's stare
shamed sad and morose
he seemed to me a man of questions
who regretted deeply the dearth
of answers to be found

[23] 6 November 2009, Qal'a-i-Najil, Mehtar Lam.

Duhkha[24]

Sans Shield[25]

all mothers always stand
stiff and proud
for all the world to see
but all mothers have always longed
to whisper to all sons
sans shield is fine
just return to me

---

[25] Either with your shield, or on it.
   Plutarch, *Sayings of Spartan Women*

One Hard Frost

late sunlight sifts the trees
shining almost sideways now
brushing cedar fronds
and a pine's soft spreading boughs
and casting bottle-brush spruce
in stark hard relief

here there and again
by some strange luck the sun slips by
between bough and bole
through needle and twig
past sprig and shoot
then it pools up on last year's leaves,
brown or buff or tan
and even though they're long since dead
the light sets all alike aglow

there are no fresh green leaves
winter still clutches the land
buds have formed on oak
on maple cherry and on apple
but they lack the warmth
to swell and burst

one hard frost will kill them all

the smoke I'm making rises
shifting cold through the needles
through the branches fronds and boughs
here and there
the shafts of sunshine
filter sideways through the billows
blistering soft evening glow

to the hard raw red of inelastic burns
desperate for an escharotomy

there is no such incision to be made
that will spring open
relieve
release the choking tightness
now settled in my chest
my luck's run out
and so I stand beside my blackened metal barrel
and one by one
flick memories into its burning maw
the smoke rises
curls drifts and sifts between the trees
unfurling acrid banners
that the sun shines reddened through

here's a wedding shot
my wife in white with glowing skin
and there's a goofy family group
the four of us all heaped up
piled on the floor
fishing pics go in
and action shots of our young twins
their sixth birthday
two wicked grins
side by side in a carnival bumper car

last of all
my phone is eaten by the barrel
a pointless gesture
burning the messenger won't reverse
the news it carried to my ear
the state trooper's quiet voice
—there'd been a crash—
and before I even dared to ask

answering the all-important question:
there were no survivors

Desert Rain

living spring leaves
spin down singly
or drift in droves
freed not by fall's frost
but snipped from trees
by snapping bullets
buzzing past

peaceful puffy clouds
beyond the boughs
reflect faintly from a face
whose skin is pallid
pouring sweat
a sallow fallen leaf
so pinched in pain
that prayers
spoken softly
ask not for survival
but beg swift passage past
this fragile failing state

from above hot salt rain
drops drips onto the pale face
and patters crater impacts
in the powdered desert dust
beside the shell that's just become
my brother's body

Death on an ODA[26]

we stand together
mute measured ranks sweating under sun
gray crunchy gravel scrunching
when weight shifts
from one burning desert boot
to the other
decked out in down range best
funeral attire
camouflage battle dress
subjected to starch and pressed
of all the damndest things

we stand together
choking off chest-ripping sobs
shoulders shaking
silent tears trickling rills through beards
and tickling chins
before drip-dropping into dust
until the speeches end
then one by one slouch forward
to kneel before the boots
the dog tags
the M4
and the picture
placed in lieu of our dead friend
though somehow
in his honor

I myself stagger forth
flop down
gouge both knees
on dusty splintered gravel
and totum corpus quaking gasp

[26] 2 August 2009, Camp Vose, Kabul.

—goodbye brother
I—
shake my head
and stand again

we stand together afterwards
while men wide-eyed at my grief
file past
each one shocked and praying to avoid
such a fate as mine
they grasp our hands and mumble sorries
while struggling to meet our eyes

we stand together later still
flipping through pictures of our friend's farewell
not one shows me
having bared my scoured plane
before a hundred men
my team stepped in as editors
and vanished my pain from posterity

I cannot recall who spoke that day
nor the names or faces even
of the men who shook our hands
but I remember my team
and how we stood together

Pater Familias

step father comes back
a different man
he comes back
angry
he used to yell
sure
on occasion
but now he looses all control
slaps   walls
punches   doors

his truck idles in the driveway
that growling V-8 as much a threat
as a high-grass rattlesnake buzz
when searching for a baseball
as thunder
on a birthday party afternoon

I could go
it rumbles
I could roll away
and leave your mother here
alone
in this mess of a life

but he's inside
jerking about
opening and slamming doors
muttering to himself
like a pissed-on bear
some little thing has set him off
I doubt even he knows what
and now once again
his truck is growling

No Rolling, Shrink

I like you
you seem friendly enough
and I've tried my damnedest to relate to you
the truth
for example
it's true *I* came to *you*
but I came for pharmacy
and lethe
not because I want help rolling
I can roll my own
thank you very much
but still
no matter how long a cavern's fetid contents
have been left to lie and fester
some rocks should never be pushed aside
some dark miracles should be forever left unseen

behind my stone you see
smolder unborn nightmares
and gravid memories
and cold imaginings
brothers buried
grave with my guilt and fear
neurotic worries for my son's soul
cowardice shame and that nameless male lack
call it unsatisfied animal lust
that underlies a plethora of human tragedies
all fertilized by my complete and utter
decaying existential hopelessness

such are my antichristic afflictions
and just so are they so unsafely tombed
but my weary ribby cart horse sense

of self preservation
implores this pestilence stay sealed up
no risk to *you* if we should choose
to press on breathing life into my dead
exposing them to unkind light
by my naming of their names

The Me I Have Become[27]

we've paddled a grenade's throw
or less
and already we're in trouble
the canoe spins on the lake like a light leaf
blown by a reeling drunken wind

I try to stay patient
offer instruction
try widening your grip
encouragement
you're doing much better now
simple advice
keep your back straight
and an anecdote or two
about my first paddling experience
I splashed so hard
I say
folks thought I was drowning a raccoon
with my paddle

I don't mention I was six at the time

roiled water lies in lazy curves behind us
but somehow
having covered the half a mile twice
we've made the crossing
now
gliding into the narrow outlet stream
I'm laughing
but still trying my damnedest
to keep it sounding cheerful

the channel squeezes tight

[27] For Kna

twists
turns
seems to spiral through the lilies
a dark ribbon at the end of a stick
flicked and curled back and forth
through a verdant sky

we bash into one bank
then carom off the other
first his strokes are too powerful
then too timid
either we make too much way
or none at all

I try to stay patient

then the walls of water lilies close
like a swamp-sized venus fly trap

we disembark and slog ahead
through weeds and noisome mud
dragging the canoe
then slop back in
relaunch
only to repeat
there are many slips
many falls
splashes
curses

I give up on being patient
not consciously of course
but the live wire I can't control
is twisting
spitting sparks
By myself I haul the canoe ahead

allowing him more time
for his useless muddy floundering

Finally I snap
and ask him how at twenty eight years old
even a city boy can be so useless in a pinch

like all swamps ambushes and adventures
this one ends too
we reach open water
the canoe drifts forward silently
we sit exhausted
coated in stinking mud
counting our itchy bug bites

I'm sorry
he says
timidly

you're sorry?
I'm the one who should be sorry
you could be my little brother
or even my young son
how could I ever justify
being so impatient with my brother or my son?
you could even be my teammate
the one I couldn't save in that mud-bloody *wadi*
when he wouldn't live
I grew impatient with him too
No
I say
I'm the one who should be sorry

except I don't say it
I can't
if I could speak such an apology

I'd have been able to hold my tongue and temper
in the first place
if I were able to speak
and keep from speaking
I would not be the me
I have become

Gondollied[28]

[28] An der Brücke stand
jüngst ich in brauner Nacht.
Fernher kam Gesang;
goldener Tropfen quoll's
über die zitternde Fläche weg.
Gondeln, Lichter, Musik -
trunken schwamm's in die Dämmrung hinaus ...

Meine Seele, ein Saitenspiel,
sang sich, unsichtbar berührt,
heimlich ein Gondellied dazu,
zitternd vor bunter Seligkeit.
—*Hörte ihr jemand zu?*
                    Friedrich Nietzsche (italics added)

I'm Still Here

Bullet
who slapped rock zipped up burrowed through my thigh[29]
and Rocket
who blasted dirt desert rock coarse grit inside my calf[30]
you came to be before
I reached desert crossed wadi climbed mountain
before I ever saw my first child
before I ever saw my first child burning
beside a VBIED-thrashed fuel blivet
burning
but alive
before my friend gasping pain sweating scared stinking iron
bled rust across my thighs
and died
before
I could not save him.[31]

you and me
violent sons sprung from peaceful lands
you and me
smuggled over desert's sands
over wadis
over mountain passes
by night
by moonlight
by cautious and determined men
you and me
laid down like seeds
by these constant men
poked into dusty soil
watered blood and fed belief
so we might sprout one day and blossom future deaths
for these stained souls

[29] 29 July 2009 (again).
[30] 5 September 2009.
[31] And again 29 July 2009. VBIED rhymes with *see kid*

these true flag thrashing believers
these oh so righteous and determined men

I've fulfilled their unthought out intent
a dozen dozen times I've interred as they intended
so many
too too many

I'm still here

but where are *you*
beside the bits residing in my leg?
my scars all scream
you've failed

Apoca Lips

they're crooning underlying panic
frantic
over breeding
stressed out mothers
an unconscious struggle for survival
a vague feeling of threat
fearing what's coming
implacable
pitiless
brutal

they're singing increasing disconnect
quantity
versus value
want versus need
control dressed impeccably as freedom
learning decked out in
brash cleverness
for the fall
season

they're chanting the coming correction
war
corona
or zombies
various means justified by an end
inevitable
necessary[32]
wavering
not at
all

[32] ...the best way out is always through.
And I agree to that, or in so far
As that I can see no way out but through–
Leastways for me...
Robert Frost, *A Servant to Servants* (italics added)

After (*a benediction*)

Afghans
cut your fields
and put away your guns

bullets are as poor as scythes
as torsos homes
for bullets

Living

a bullet slaps a rock a handspan from your knee
spraying little needles up to sliver in your leg[33]
or a round whiffs past your head and smacks into a tree
gouging out a hole and raining splinters on your egg[34]

or you're lying cringing prone
in a wavy naked field
with bullets clipping grass stems
like a probing florist's scissors[35]

or you're shaded while the Moirai
prune the nearby somber trees
dropping twigs down on your neck
leaving leaves stuck in your sweat[36]

or a bomb rips off too soon
before your truck draws close
a dark flash and one big boom
and a spraying of debris[37]

or your eyeballs press the window
of the heli sent to lift you from a tracer laser show
wait while the others load waiting waiting waiting waiting
while in the outer dark the muj are aiming

and through the plexiglass you see a fat red donut RPG
and just before the donut eats your flying taxi
straining lifting heavy off the mountain
it impacts on a rock beneath
and showers sparks up in a fountain—[38]

[33] 29 July 2009 again. Where were *you*?
[34] Again. Where *were* you?
[35] And again. *Where* were you?
[36] And again; where were you?
[37] 4 July 2008, just outside FOB Kutschbach in the Tagab Valley. Any IEDs on *your* Independence Day that year?
[38] 0030, 5 September 2009, a hilltop just south of Hendor, Methar Lam. You?

just so a rippling music plays
when life breathes hot honey in your face
the flat dull ears
of wasted time and drear existences
are stone to higher melodies
to living life and dying death alike

First Incision

after meds
talking
vision quests
and meditation
the rock remains unbalanced
the ice rotten
set to give

so trembling I begin my work at this new cure
knowing no more of singing
than a leaf knows of frost
or a heart
a bullet

the scalpel draws across the forehead
the skin springs apart
blood is dabbed
vessels cauterized
front and top of skull
are sawn through[39]
then removed and placed
for safe keeping
within the body's natural environment
i.e. inside this patient's abdomen

now the gentle instruments begin to probe
now the disparate lobes are reapproximated
but no neurosurgeon this
the work
confused by the necessary use of two mirrors
perception and memory
progresses or fails to progress
by my own unskilled hands

[39] **Concerning trephination**, when necessity compels you to trephine a patient, here is what **you must know**: if you trephine, having undertaken (the patient's) care from the beginning, **you should not** excise the bone down to the membrane straightaway. For **(I)t is not good** for the membrane **to be bare** of bone **and subject**

to remain truthful
to honor my dead friend
and myself
I can make no mistakes

mistakes are made
hesitant starts
restarts
turnings wrong and less wrong
approximation of my scattered shattered bits of brain
progresses in fits
between fits partially brought on by this
my endeavoring to fix my fits

frustration
agony
in short
learning
become my daily bread
and there's every chance such mana won't sustain
the skull segment might remain
forever a cradled refugee inside my peritoneum
my pia mater might never be drawn together
my gray matter might stay scattered and diffuse

no cure guaranteed
no healthy outcome assured
only further struggle
and a chance of measured
most likely minimal
betterment
yet I *will* persist in singing forth
my as-yet still roiling past

to damaging **exposure** for a long time; otherwise it may finally become macerat-
ed. **And** there is **also** another danger that, if you trephine down to the membrane
and at once remove the bone, **you may**, in the procedure, **damage** the membrane
with **the** trephine.

Hippocrates, Concerning Head (w)ounds

epilogue:

- speech or short poem addressed to spectators after the conclusion of a play to convey a sentiment, describe the general mood, or give voice to a specific character's mindset. For example, in various of his play's epilogues, Shakespeare wrote

>the rain it raineth every day
>Twelfth Night

and

>A glooming peace this morning with it brings
>Romeo and Juliet

but also

>what strength I have's mine own
>The Tempest

- the concluding part of a literary work

The Ambush

this is the part where I'm supposed to give a speech
to mumble a few kind words of thanks
gracious and humble and enthusiastic
this is the part I've been waiting for

this is the part where all you wonderful people
realize this speech is a poem
hmmm you think
how unconventional!

this is the part where I pull out a fucking pistol
uh-oh
and blow off my own fucking head
at this podium
in this fucking church
in front of all you wonderful fucking people

be shocked
be outraged
be incensed
be disgusted
be insulted
wallow
in this moment
relearn
to revel in your feelings

then leave the island
this island
your island

whatever lump of land you've fortified
and strike out
into fear
into disgust
into outrage
and live   live   live

strive
to be so angry
hope
to be so loved

Acknowledgements

I would like to give heartfelt thanks to the wonderful teachers and poets who helped make his work what it is today—Ben Friedlander, Jennifer Moxley, and Carol Ann Davis. And thank you as well to Mr. Matt Winkler—without your vision and belief these poems might have remained forever smothered under the snowflakes.

About the Author

Ryan Stovall is a former adventurer, world traveler, and Green Beret twice decorated for valor and awarded two Purple Hearts. Since returning from Pakistan in 2016 he has found writing to be a therapeutic outlet for coping with PTSD. His poetry won the 2018 Wright Award from Line of Advance and has appeared in Rosebud, The Cape Rock, Here Comes Everyone, and other journals and anthologies. Ryan writes and lives with his family in Western Maine.